MY WORLD OF DREAMS

TIRADE – MY TIRADE

Yes, this is my tirade.

If you are not used to my writing; know that I can, and do go off reckless and rude in some of these books.

This book is truly no exception as I did go off reckless, and rude.

As usual; I make no apologies. I have to let off steam, and I did in a brutal way.

Listen people; my true family. Writing is also my way of releasing my negative energy when people piss me off. It matters not if it's humans or, someone who is dead.

You have your avenue of dealing with negative people and forces, and I have my way.

I refuse to pick up arms and fight. My victory are these books and yes, **hell.**

You want to open the door to hell; let me help you, and close it behind you. Once the door is closed, I am not going to open the door for you to get out. There you go; death; that individual and or, nation is all yours. Good riddance; that evil is gone infinitely and indefinitely more than forever ever without end.

Michelle
February 10, 2019

FULFILLMENT TIME TONY TUFF FEAT. SMOKIE BENZ

The world; well people of the world has, and have gone crazy. Demons roam the earth at will, and kill at will.

More mental issues plaguing humans globally.

Aye sah, what a state humans are in.

Yes, my dream world has, and have been quiet as of late, and this is truly good for me.

It's February 4, 2019, and I feel as if I am in my own little world that is void of the outside world; other humans.

In my world; I don't have to think about other humans, nor do their life affect me. I truly do not see them; no longer see their destruction, and ills of the world.

Yes, the spiritual world has, and have changed for me, and I will forever tell you, I am sleeping better. No destruction. Death in this way is calm.

Oh man, I can't remember if I dreamt Kim and Kanye West; with Kim throwing her shoe at and or, after him. Shoe for me is truly not good. So I have to wait and see if by the end of the year and or, months, or years to come if they divorce. But if in fact I did see this; Kim throwing her shoe at Kanye then they are going to separate; divorce, and it will not be a pretty divorce, but a messy one.

Dreamt Selassie; the dead Ethiopian King. Family, and people; my true family. This man dream mi. He wanted to join me. I categorically told him no in my dream, and woke up out of my dream world, and reiterated my no in my waking state so that the physical, and spiritual realm know for a fact without doubt that I truly, more than infinitely, and indefinitely; more than forever ever without end, truly; categorically truly; Lovey truly do not want this man in my realm; world, world with Lovey, dream world, anywhere near me period, and more.

Of all the people; him. Scunthole leave me alone. I deny you without doubt. I truly know you not so stay in hell. Your home is already prepared in hell for you, and I will not take you out of hell. Stay the hell there and burn. You joined the forces of evil; your people turned from Lovey long ago anna mi fi save yu. Kiss my natural brown ass. Dyam sell out. Dyam careless Ethiopian.

Life is real. There is a good and true place in Lovey's realm for the children and people of truth; life. Your people forfeited life when your ancestors joined Babylon, and accepted the nastiness of Babylon. ***THEREFORE; YOUR LAND, AND PEOPLE FORFEITED THE ARC OF THE COVENANT; LIFE.*** So truly don't come to me wanting to join me because, I would forever ever **NEVER** <u>forfeit my place, and stay with Lovey for you, or your people; any Babylonian, or otherwise period.</u>

MY WORLD OF DREAMS 2019 – BOOK THREE - TIRADE

Ethiopia lost their place with God for whom I call Lovey, and it's going to stay that way in my book, and world. I refuse to; categorically with every truth in the world, universe, Lovey's world, my world, and beyond, refuse to save you, your land, and people. Kick rocks, and suffer your damned condemned faith, and leave me the bleep alone.

No saving grace for you, your land, and your people, and eternity, and every human whether living, or dead can take these words, and bank on them as being my full and true truth for you, your children, and people, ancestors, land, and kingdom including future. Bleep off, and truly do not find me again. You're a bleeping disgrace, and condemnation of life.

Lovey saw it befitting to walk away from the lots of you, and I'm to defy, and defile Lovey for you? Bitch kick rocks literally, and bleep the bleep off.

You are BC death so stay dead literally.

Dyam wrenk fi cum fine mi. who yu?

Yu a anybody.

Listen bitch, mi annuh Rasta.
Mi nuh Ras.
Mi a nuh Tafari

Dem; di Rastas of the world; globe kiss your ass. I am the one to tell you; F you, and sit and hold my peace, and I am literally telling you in death because you are dead to; F you. And if you were alive, I would tell you the same damned thing to Kiss my ass, and F you, and by me writing these worlds you are told in life, and in death to; F you, and kiss my natural brown ass.

Burn in hell bitch. Bleeping sell out. Yu si yu hell now, suh you want me to save you from hell. MORE FIYAH I say.

Save you….cunnumunnu; leave me alone. *I am not a careless Ethiopian* because, our Black Ancestors made sure they reminded us of the saying of you, and your people. They kept the saying; **CARELESS ETHIOPIAN FOR US TO REMEMBER NOT TO SELL OUT GOD AND OR, LOVEY LIKE YOUR PEOPLE DID LONG AGO.**

Therefore, I know death, and every Ras; Rasta, is death.

RAS, RASTA, TAFARI, RASTAFARI is death; physical death.

WHEN A RASTA SAY THEY ARE RASTA, RASTAFARI; THEY ARE ACKNOWLEDGING DEATH. THEY ARE TELLING ALL OF HUMANITY, AND GOD; THE GOD OF LIFE THAT; THEY ARE APART OF THE REALM, WORLD, AND PEOPLE OF DEATH. THEY'VE ACCEPTED BLACK DEATH AS THEIR SAVIOUR, KING, GOD, AND ALL.

RASTA IS BLACK DEATH – THE ONE TO TAKE YOUR SOUL AND OR, SPIRIT, AND HAND IT OVER TO DEATH; WHITE DEATH TO DIE.

Therefore, **BLACK AND WHITE DEATH.**

WHEN YOU SEE A RASTA; FEMALE, OR MALE BLACK RASTA; YOU ARE SEEING WHAT BLACK DEATH TRULY LOOK LIKE. SO TRULY DON'T WITH ME BECAUSE I SEE BEYOND YOU BITCH.

And yes, you Black Rastas; all Rasta is going to come after me for this, but truth is truth. This is who you are, and this is who you shall forever be. BLACK DEATH.

Therefore, many of you in the Black Race pick up other people's culture, embrace it, defend it, without knowing what the hell you defend.

Therefore, hundreds of millions of you DEFEND DEATH WITHOUT KNOWING IT.

FOOL, FOOL, BLACK PEOPLE, NOT ALL AFRICANS IS OF GOD, AND NOT ALL AFRICA LAND IS OF GOD.

NOT ALL OF AFRICA WILL BE SAVED THEREFORE, KNOW THE TRUTH, AS WELL AS;

YOUR FULL, AND TRUE HISTORY, AND LIFE STORY.

And any Rasta come after me for this; the door, and doors of hell is open for you, and to you.

I will close it behind you especially you the fool, fool Jamaican ones that truly do not know who you are, or what Jamaica stand for. Dyam falla batty nuff a unnu.

It's a shame it had to take you this long since your physical death to find your home in hell. In my book; your ass should have been in hell long ago burning alongside your sell out ancestors. Thus, hell is not right away for some spirit; once your flesh shed the spirit.

Yes family and people; my true family, I had to do a mini vent. Wey di yass dis man a fine mi fa? Mi noa im?

Therefore, I tell you the spiritual world and or, realm has changed. Something is happening spiritually that I truly cannot figure out.

Like I said in book one; I truly do not know if this is the calm before the storm.

I know I have petitioned Lovey to exclude the White Race off our good and true mountain of life, but you know what; Lovey truly do not listen to me.

MY WORLD OF DREAMS 2019 – BOOK THREE - TIRADE

To me, and for me; Lovey cannot see the damage these people; White People based on hue, and based on hue and evil deeds has, and have done to this earth, the people of this earth, the environment of earth, spiritual realm, and so much more.

Death, and Lovey have man's so called Holy Book; Bible as a testament of how lie, and deceitful these people are. Yet, both Lovey, and Death fail to punish these people. Meaning, Lovey refuse to walk away from them in goodness, and in truth.

They; White People, make people believe they are true when they lie, and deceive; steal; kill. They go against every fabric, and energy of life; good and true life, and Lovey cannot see this therefore, I will not save them; wicked and evil White People.

<u>*Yes; many Blacks are wicked too, but if ever I tell you. SOME BLACKS ARE WHITE, AND SOME WHITES ARE BLACK.*</u>

<u>*In life; Lovey and or, God cannot base life; good and true life off/on hue; skin colour. Lovey must base life off the good you do, and the good and true truth you live by.*</u>

I've told you time and time again:

NO ONE CAN TAKE COLOUR; HUE AND OR, THE COLOUR OF ONE'S SKIN TO LOVEY; GOD. YOU WILL NOT GET ANYWHERE.

LOVEY TRULY DO NOT SEE YOU, AND WILL NEVER SEE YOU.

Life is truly not skin colour therefore, I truly do not know why people hate based on skin tone.

YOUR SKIN TONE REPRESENT THE DIFFERENT DEATHS.
Is a reminder of physical, and spiritual death.

BLACK SKIN REPRESENT BLACK DEATH. PHYSICAL DEATH. HE WHO TAKES YOUR SPIRIT AND HAND IT OVER TO WHITE DEATH.

This is where Rastas come in. When you see a BLACK RASTA not White, but Black Rasta, you are seeing what the Death Angel that take your spirit from your flesh look like literally.

WHITE SKIN REPRESENT FINAL DEATH AND OR, SPIRITUAL DEATH; with spiritual death being for the wicked and evil of this earth. So, if you are black, and you are evil; you die as white dressed in white in the spiritual realm; well hell. This you can take to the bank because, this is the full and true truth. This is how I saw it, and this is how I am relating it back to you. So when people are hating based on colour, I see death hating on death.

BLACK DEATH CANNOT KILL YOU, ONLY WHITE DEATH CAN.

YOU'RE BOTH GOING TO DIE IN THE SAME PLACE; HELL.

Oh man, I so can't remember if I was on another planet therefore, the turmoil of humans here on earth is real.

Just this morning I dreamt hair. This male hairdresser made this Black Girl's hair Platinum Blonde; full white; bob cut; short. Her air looked nice, but I said; I did not like it. I wanted her to have her natural kinky hair, and he took out the Platinum Blonde, and gave her her natural gold black brown hair for which I loved. and wanted my hair to be that way. But, the weird part of the dream was. My hair he made Platinum Blonde with brown; red brown I would say going down the middle of my head. Also, the Platinum Blonde part of my hair had curls; was curly, and nice.

So yes, I have to watch my health keenly. I know the issues with my health, and I so have to get my health in check. I am so not taking care of myself people. I truly need to be in the right environment for me.

MY WORLD OF DREAMS 2019 – BOOK THREE - TIRADE

I need to cut a lot of things out of my life, and processed sugar is truly one of them. I am addicted to sugar, and this is so not good.

Yes, my dream world is on a mini vacation, and this is so good for me because I am truly sleeping better.

I better go now, but truly think of me. Good thoughts only please.

Hey, we are each other's good rescue.

I know you may not understand, but in life some of us do need rescuing, and if I can rescue you the good and true that need rescuing then; let us rescue each other.

The battle or fire rages, but we will make it.

THERE IS AN END TO EVIL, BUT LIFE; GOOD AND TRUE LIFE CANNOT END.

RIDE NATTY RIDE by Robert Nesta Marley aka Bob Marley. I know many of you will not get this song, but for those who are true spiritualist will know what he, Bob Marley is talking about, and educating you on. He told you to: "KNOW AND NOT BELIEVE."

NEVER FORGOT OUR FIRE FOR THE WICKED AND EVIL IS HELL.

No one can escape hell. Therefore, BE OF GOOD COURAGE no matter how touch the road, and your way is.

Evil is but for a time, but good and true life is forever ever; cannot end. Nor is good and true life for a time.

So come on and LIVELY UP YOURSELF Bob Marley.

Michelle
February 4, 2019

MY WORLD OF DREAMS 2019 – BOOK THREE - TIRADE

I totally forgot it's Black History Month.

So to all the Black Creators of the past, present, and future; Happy Black History Month. Well, **_BLACK TRUTH MONTH._** Without you all, this earth would not be in existence. So; true peace, and blessing be unto all of you. Truly do forgive me for forgetting. Hey, we have the truest month of the calendar year to celebrate all of you.

To the Black Creators of this world both great, and small thank you for creating beauty in me, and around me.

Yes, it's sad humans are destroying the beauty you gave us, but in my heart; true heart, we will create anew. We must create anew.

Oh, if only your good and true world was mine right now.

YOUR WORLD OR MINE by Luciano the reggae artist.

True love always, and once again, thank you for creation because I know for a fact there were no WHITE CREATORS, and this makes me prouder than proud. I know many may say I am racist, but I truly don't give a damn. I am BLACK AND MORE THAN PROUD OF ME, AND CREATION; OUR BLACK CREATORS AND DESIGNERS.

Yea Black People all the way.

Michelle
February 4, 2019

MY WORLD OF DREAMS 2019 – BOOK THREE - TIRADE

It's February 08, 2019, and I am listening to; **_SUCCESS STORY_** by Nesbeth. Truly love this song.

Success isn't easy for the truly trying; those that do not sell their soul to reach the top of the financial; money meat market.

So, slow and easy for me and those who truly love what they do. We have to persevere for real.

Not much to report dream wise. My dream world is on vacation which is truly good for me in many ways. I just have to watch and see the lives of humans unravel in a negative way.

Too chaos on earth when it comes to humans globally.

Too much hate, and no one truly want to stop it; thus conflict; war is in the heart of many.

Too much/many humans are fueled by hate.

Therefore; many leaders instigate hate, and you the people of the world are the cunnumunnu's that follow your demented leaders to hell.

Did I dream about the now president of the United States?

Yes

I truly cannot remember the dream apart from him being in front of a crowd.

Oh man, I cannot remember if he's the catalyst for something. No, he's not. But when it comes to rich people globally; I truly do not know what is going to happen to them. I can't remember if I saw them; no, I think it was implied; no, not implied.

You know what. I so can't remember. But rich people are going to lose it all. Which minute; year they lose it all, I truly do not know.

This world is in distress people, and this is caused by us; humans globally. Instead of preserving our life and this earth; we fuss, fight; kill **therefore; making EARTH THE HAVEN FOR THIEVES AND MURDERERS.**

Therefore, humans cannot preserve life, or this earth; they can only kill, and destroy.

Therefore, for me; nothing good came from procreation; the union of sperm, and egg.

It is going to get worse on earth, and I am truly not worried about the death toll of humans because; **HUMANS DID MAKE THE CHOICE TO KILL.**

HUMANS DID MAKE THE CHOICE TO LIVE IN HATE.

HUMANS DID MAKE THE CHOICE TO HATE EACH OTHER.

HUMANS DID MAKE THE CHOICE TO LIE, AND LIVE BY LIES.

HUMANS DID MAKE THE CHOICE TO BE STRIFE DRIVEN.

HUMANS DID MAKE THE CHOICE TO BELIEVE INSTEAD OF KNOW.

HUMANS DID MAKE THE CHOICE TO LET EVIL; ALL MANNER OF EVIL REIGN HERE ON EARTH. SO, HOW HUMANS DIE CONCERNS ME NOT.

YOU MADE THE CHOICE TO DIE; SO LIVE BY YOUR CHOICE OF DEATH PERIOD.

Dreaming more and more about SG. Yea me.

Comfort yes, but no. Spirituality, amongst other things documented in earlier books. SG is a forbidden fruit for me.

Walk with me people; my good and true family.

Oh my Lord we so need to go for a walk. No march because; I refuse to march for people that sell out life, cause chaos and strife in the lives of others, go into forbidden land and lands, war with others, use politics and religion to kill, and take life from life. Shit, I refuse heroics. Being dumb and stupid do not make you an hero.

I refuse to give up my life for, or to anyone. Why the hell should I sacrifice my sweet and good up good up life for anyone? Not even Lovey I would give up my life for.

Nope. You cause strife with others; come out of it on your own. No one told you to create strife with your neighbour. However, if your neighbour is creating strife with you, and your good and true desire is to move out of the neighbourhood, and I can help you to do so good and true in true peace, then I will help you if I can.

No one should live in misery. Nor should you build the land and or, environment you are miserable in.

Change your mindset.

Yes there is more but I am going to leave things as is.

Michelle

MY WORLD OF DREAMS 2019 – BOOK THREE - TIRADE

It's February 10th, and my dream world is still relatively calm.

Am I loving this calmness?

Yes, but the dead still find me. I am so not going to worry about the dead because I cannot save them from hell.

Black people are dying thus; I am seeing the faces of female, and male black people who are going to die shortly.

And no, I still do not wish I was an artist to draw the faces I see when I close my eyes.

This morning did I dream Hilary Clinton?

Yes

She was doing a commercial for CPAP Machines. Apparently, they had new masks that did not allow so much force and or, pressure going into your nasal passage. This would be good, because even with the lowest setting they have, people like me have issues with the pressure going into my nostrils.

Hideous contraption that I wish they would re-invent.

Oh well, people have to sell shit I guess. I literally loathe that machine due to my horrible experience with it. But hey, my loathing the contraption have, and has absolutely nothing to do with you, it has all to do with me.

Expensive junk I call it; the CPAP Machine.

So, hopefully, something new will be coming out for this machine where it's better, simpler to use, and not so hideous. God, I am so glad I do not have a mate because with that contraption; it's as if you are in a scary movie.

God; wow.

Yes, I know the flow is off in this book, but bare with me please.

I truly do not know what to say about this one. I was not dreaming in my view. But it's as if I was awake, and dreaming at the same time. It's weird because I do not know if there is dream wake sleep, or dreaming, and waking up at the same time.

Oh man, I truly do not know if that make any sense in the spiritual, and real world. I was with this Black Man. He was a driver, and I asked why were Jamaican's so wicked? No, I was thinking about the wickedness of Jamaicans in the living; how dem; Jamaicans suh vile and wicked. He too was asking and or saying how Jamaicans were so wicked. He never told me why because it was a sleep wake dream if that make any sense.

So yes, there is something wicked possessing the people of Jamaica, and I am so not going to worry about it. **LOVEY DID TELL ME THE ISLAND WAS UNCLEAN.** Therefore, I am truly not going to worry myself about unclean people. The vileness of the people to each other will never change, and is truly not going to change with what's happening in the country. Jamaica

I REFUSE TO WORRY ABOUT THE PEOPLE OF THE LAND, BECAUSE THEY ARE THE ONES TO CAUSE THIS ON SELF. ABSOLUTELY NOT ONE THINK OF THEIR ACTIONS.

Who nuh sacrifice, Obeah. Yes some do both, but blood haffi run inna lickle Jamaica because the people, and the politicians, including religious leaders set it so.

Death must walk, and claim lives in that land. Therefore, mek dem tan. **A PEOPLE WITHOUT MORAL VALUES OR, VALUE CANNOT VALUE SELF, OR OTHERS.**

Absolutely no one in Jamaica value self; their life, and the life of others therefore; they do the shit they do not just in Jamaica, but globally.

Therefore, NO ONE CAN TELL ME ABOUT SLAVERY, THE SLAVE MENTALITY LEST I BLAST THEM FROM HERE TO KINGDOM COME. Truly do not make excuses with me. Tu much a dem a damn bad breed pickney. If they were not, they would not be fighting, and killing each other.

Therefore:

Politician corrupt
Pastor corrupt
Madda corrupt
Faada corrupt
Pickney corrupt
Ancestors corrupt

Suh, nuh betta barrel, nuh betta herring. Generations of corrupt and immoral devils; people. Vipers they are.

Children of Cain of their nasty book – so called holy bible. **THEY LIVE TO KILL PERIOD.**

No wonder Jamaica, and Jamaicans caane betta.

Dyam licky, licky, an red eye.

Change your mindset, and mentality. Focus on you, and making your life better instead of; grudging the next man and or, person for what they have.

Stop your bullshit because; you do not know how some people come by their fame, and fortune.

No unnu noa but refuse to say. Therefore, many a unnu live a obeah man an oman fi real.

So yes, the spiritual world have to talk, and they are talking, and asking.

Jamaica, and Jamaicans; what went wrong?

No Jamaica tell me; what happened?

What went wrong on land, and in spirit for Jamaicans to be so vile and wicked to self, and others?

Who cursed the land, and people of Jamaica falsely?

What curse is on the land, and people for Jamaicans to behave – guane so terribly?

Laade Gad man; people can vile suh?

Unnu need betta days.

A NEW DAY *by the reggae artist Luciano. Truly; Jamaica, and the people of Jamaica need to be cleansed physically, and spiritually.*

Jamaicans can no longer live immorally.

MY WORLD OF DREAMS 2019 – BOOK THREE - TIRADE

<u>WHERE ARE THE HEARTS</u> by the reggae artist Luciano. Man this song is so true when it comes to the leaders of world. Truly love this song.

WE NEED TRUE, CLEAN, GOOD, RIGHTEOUS, AND TRULY LOVING LEADERS THAT TRULY CARE FOR THEIR LAND, AND PEOPLE.

It's time for a CHANGE; POSITIVE CHANGE. We truly do not need the lies, and deceit that is being fed to humans globally. Therefore, the heart of many is mucky; unclean fi real.

<u>CALL ME CRAZY</u> by Jah Sun. Nice song and beat. Yep I am bumping to this song. Goh dey Jah Sun.

<u>LOVE CURRENCY</u> by Jah Sun

<u>JOURNEY OF 1000 MILES</u> by Jah Sun

<u>LIFE WE LIVE</u> by Jah Cure

<u>CHANT DOWN BABYLON</u> by Bob Marley. You truly do not need violence to defeat your enemy, and enemies. Positive thinking, good, and positive music, positive reasoning, true and unchangeable knowledge. Vibration – positive vibration is one of the keys.

<u>TOO BEGGY BEGGY</u> by Bugle

Goh dey Bugle. Laade this is so true. When yu tell some a dem fi goh plant some food; dem tell yu sey dem han too clean. Yet dem a look fi hand out.

Some dey pan street corner a med how fi rab yu, and snuff out yu life. Big Tune Bugle, big tune.

Shout out to J. Boog

<u>WORTH MY TIME</u> by J. Boog

<u>GOOD CRY</u> by J. Boog featuring Chaka Demus.
Truly love this song fi more than real. Makes you want to bubble all the way. Up, up, up. Have to buy on iTunes.
Pull Up, and rewind to the max missa selecta. Brap, brap

Wow, my day was going great, and I was having so much fun, and dancing crazy mad in my chair to; **GOOD CRY by J. Boog and Chaka Demus;** then my brother called to ruin my day, and year so far with his DNA BULLSHIT.

Come tell me bout his daughter did a DNA of our ancestry. Don't come tell me crap about 30% of our heritage and or, ancestry is SYRIAN. I REBUKE YOU IN THE GOOD, AND TRUE NAME OF LOVEY, AND MY GORGEOUS AND BEAUTIFUL MOTHER. KEEP YOUR DNA BULLSHIT BECAUSE I WILL NEVER EVER ACCEPT THAT SHIT. F OFF. YOU CAN BE HAPPY ABOUT THAT SHIT, BUT NOT ME. F YOU AND YOUR SYRIAN BULLSHIT.

DNA is shit. Nothing can White People tell me, and I will acknowledge as true.

Fool fool BLACK PEOPLE LACKA UNNU CAN BUY INTO THEIR SHIT BECAUSE UNNU CAANE ACCEPT THAT UNNU A BLACK; OF LIFE, AND GOD.

I KNOW THE SPIRIT, AND THE SPIRITUAL REALM; SO TRULY DON'T COME TO ME WITH THE SYRIAN BULLSHIT BECAUSE I REBUKE YOU, AND YOUR LIES OF SHIT ROYALLY.

UNNU NUH HA NUTTIN FI DU. CUNNUMUNNU, YOU CANNOT BREAK DOWN YOUR SPIRIT. YOUR SPIRIT IS YOUR TRUE LIFE THEREFORE, DNA IS SHIT. NO HUMAN BEING ON THE FACE OF THIS PLANET WHETHER LIVING, OR DEAD CAN MAP YOUR SPIRIT, OR TELL WHERE IN YOUR PHYSICAL BODY THE SPIRIT IS. SO TRULY DON'T WITH ME.

I KNOW LIFE. YOUR FLESH IS NOT LIFE; SO COME AGAIN WHEN IT COMES TO ME WITH LIFE. YOU MAY NEED TO BELONG HENCE, YOU ARE HAPPY ABOUT HAVING 30% SYRIAN IN YOU, **AND THIS IS YOUR RIGHT.** HENCE LOVEY KNOW ME. F SYRIA – BABYLON. I TRULY DO NOT ASSOCIATE MYSELF WITH THEM, AND REFUSE TO.

HENCE; BUN BABYLON AND THEIR SINFUL, AND DEMENTED WAYS, AND PEOPLE.

I CARE NOT FOR THEM HENCE; **ALL OF BABYLON WAS, AND STILL IS LOCKED OUT OF LIFE.** SO, IF YOU

WANT TO BE LOCKED OUT OF LIFE; CONTINUE TO PROVOKE ME WITH YOUR SYRIAN BULLSHIT. I WILL ENSURE LOVEY LOCK YOUR ASS OUT OF LIFE WITH YOUR CURSE, AND CURSE OF LIFE.

FIYAH FI ALL BABYLONIANS. WHY THE HELL DO YOU THINK THERE ARE NO BABYLONIANS ON LOVEY'S AND OR, GOD'S GOOD, AND TRUE MOUNTAIN?

TO GO BACK TO MARTIN LUTHER KING JR. DID HE NOT SAY; TELL THE LOTS OF YOU ABOUT BE MOUNTAIN. Jews and Gentiles

HE DID NOT SEE ANY BABYLONIAN ON GOD'S GOOD, AND TRUE MOUNTAIN THUS; HIS SPEECH ABOUT HIM BEING ON THE MOUNTAIN OF GOD. LEARN.

Better yet, go back to man's nasty book called the Holy Bible back in the time of Moses.

What did Moses see when he came from the top of the Mountain after conversing with God?

Was it not Babylon; Babylonian Indians that got Blacks to worship, and bow down to their Golden Calf?

<u>Who worship the cow until this day?</u>

Because of what Babylon did to Black People, Moses had to exclude all of Babylon from life. Just like I've done; asked Lovey for when it comes to WICKED AND EVIL WHITE PEOPLE GLOBALLY. Thus, many until this day say; MOSES BROKE GOD'S COMMANDMENT.

Moses didn't break God's commandment; Moses kept the devil's children from entering ZION; GOD'S KINGDOM. Know the truth. This is why Babylon; Indians; all of Babylon will forever hate BLACK PEOPLE. Yes, there is more, but I am going to leave it there. Babylon will forever get you the idiot Blacks of the globe to lose your place in God's Kingdom.

DYAM EDIAT FI REAL.

WE AS BLACK PEOPLE ARE TOO BLEEPING GULLIBLE. WE ARE QUICK TO JUMP ON WHAT THE ENEMY TELL US, AND ACCEPT THE SHIT THEY GIVE US, AND SAY IT'S THE TRUTH. NO ONE CAN MAP YOUR LIFE EDIAT.

IF MAN COULD MAP YOUR LIFE, THEY WOULD FIND GOD.

THEY WOULD KNOW YOU.

WHAT WILL HAPPEN IN YOUR LIFE NEXT.

IF MAN COULD MAP YOUR LIFE, ***THEY WOULD BE ABLE TO MAP THE LIFE OF GOD.***

IF MAN COULD MAP YOUR LIFE, ***THEY WOULD FIND TIME; TRUE TIME, AND TIME IN TIME.***

Listen you are my brother, but do not let me go off on you reckless and rude. I truly do not need to belong to any culture. **<u>I am of Scot; therefore, I know physical, and spiritual life.</u>**

<u>I am a true Jamaican therefore, I was born of life, and know life.</u>

My mother did not know her father because; **<u>the scumbag</u>** *fool up our grandmother. He could not, and never stood up to his responsibility as a father therefore, I DO NOT CLAIM HIS LINEAGE UNDER ANY CIRCUMSTANCES AND YES, I CAN DO THIS.*

My beautiful and gorgeous mother never spoke to us of **<u>this degenerate – worse than scumbag and sperm donor</u>** *so; why are you bleeping proud to acknowledge his lineage?*

A true man/father stand up to his, and her responsibility as a father.

A true man/father is there for his, and her children.

A true man/father ensures the needs and wants of his, and her children are met.

A true man/father teaches his, and her children good moral values.

A true man/father do not cut, or walk out of his/her children life. They ensure they are there for them.

A true man/father raise their/his and or, her children right. Therefore, his/her children can speak of the goodness of their father, and take these good values into the future so that they can intern teach their children, and children's children these good values.

<u>Condemned is he</u> because; if I could find him in death, I would spit in his bleeping face, and tell death to make sure every anger in me is taken out on him worse than anything he, and she death have in their arsenal of fire and death, and if they cannot then; I would create a hotter fire for this scumbag. **<u>Let the bitch of shit stay bleeping dead.</u>**

I acknowledge him not. My beautiful, and gorgeous mother was not raised by him nor did she know him in truth, and it's a good thing because; she was raised right therefore, I more than truly love her, and save her with all my truth, and blessing.

Don't want to know them because; we don't know him, and I have truly and truthfully disowned him, or any link to him; them.

You're my brother, but you are not true to your own mother in death, and life. Why the bleep do you seek to belong to a bleeping condemned race of people? I have Lovey, and I have my truly beautiful and gorgeous mother. She's the one I accept as mother, father, grandfather; ALL.

Watchya man, you are my brother, but truly don't let me curse you. Bury it because it's buried with me.

I am going to go this far:

<u>As for you the scum bucket of hell and earth,</u> *yes I know your name as was told by us. You B. Stewart. I do not know if you are dead or alive, I denounce you, and will never ever under any circumstance(s) acknowledge you as being a family member of mine. Eat shit, and F the hell off. I truly don't need you, or your pathetic lineage. I divorce you, and your lineage in goodness and truth.*

My gorgeous mother is my mother. You did not acknowledge her as your child hence; **<u>you fooled up my grandmother.</u>**

LET ME SAY THIS, AND TELL YOU THIS IN THE LIVING, AND DEATH. YOU HAVE ABSOLUTELY NO SAVING GRACE FROM ME, OR WITH ME WHETHER I AM THE SAVING GRACE OF HUMANITY OR NOT.

HERE, TAKE YOUR PASS FROM ME, AND GO DIRECTLY TO HELL AND BURN. THIS IS MY GOOD AND TRUE WILL OF YOU. YOU ARE NOT, AND WILL NEVER EVER BE MY GRANDFATHER OF ANY KIND OR ORIGIN. THEREFORE, YOUR LINEAGE IS TRULY NOT MY LINEAGE HENCE; I DENOUNCE YOU, AND YOUR ANCESTRY. It is written therefore, Lovey, the world, spiritual realm, and my gorgeous and beautiful mother have my good and true will.

Yes, my falla batty family members can accept you, but I refuse to accept you, and your lineage. **_I CATEGORICALLY KNOW YOU NOT._** *THEREFORE, I NEVER MET YOU IN LIFE AND DEATH, AND TRULY DON'T WANT TO EITHER.*

Yes, my beautiful mother had siblings, and I truly know them not, and refuse to know them. My mother is a part of my truth in life all around, and I TRULY HAVE TO RESPECT HER. You never respected her, or my grandmother thus; you never claimed her as your own.

You lied; fooled up my grandmother.

You weren't a man, but a piece of shit that walk, and fool up people pickney. Scumbag, I respect you not. Shit, the demons of hell have more respect in my book than you. And Lovey, and Death truly do not go there. Thus, you both including the demons of hell know my massive anger. Suh Death ole yu caana fi real.

My other siblings can acknowledge you, but I will not under any circumstance, or circumstances. I know the truth I have in you my gorgeous and beautiful mother, and I will defend you in life, and death.

Therefore, set your dumbass son straight in a good way.

First and foremost including finally. ***IF I HAD BABYLONIAN DNA. LOVEY WOULD NEVER ACKNOWLEDGE ME OR EVEN ASK ME TO WRITE A BOOK.***

So, for all you STUPID BLACK PEOPLE THAT SEEK ACCEPTANCE FOR BEING OF ANOTHER CULTURE; F THE LOTS OF YOU WITH THIS DNA BULLSHIT.

WHEN YOU CAN MAP, AND TELL ME ABOUT TRUE LIFE; THE SPIRIT THAT IS WITHIN YOUR BODY THEN TRULY COME TO ME, AND TALK.

Life originated from BLACK PEOPLE.

WE WERE THE FIRST.

ALL OF EARTH WAS ONE LAND. BUT DUE TO SIN; THE SIN AND SINS OF MEN; US AS HUMANS, EARTH BEGAN TO SPLIT; SHIFT.

CIVILIZATION STARTED WITH BLACK AND ASIAN PEOPLE THEREFORE, THERE IS NO KENYAN DNA, SOUTH AFRICAN DNA. ALL BLACK PEOPLE CAME FROM THE SAME SOURCE – BLACK MOTHER EDIAT.

AS BLACK PEOPLE STARTED TO DISOBEY GOD; GOOD AND TRUE LIFE, THEY SEPARATED FROM EACH OTHER. THIS IS WHY YOU HAVE THE DIFFERENT LANDS GLOBALLY, AND PEOPLE TAKING ON DIFFERENT IDENTITY.

MY WORLD OF DREAMS 2019 – BOOK THREE - TIRADE

Learn the truth of creation, and procreation instead of coming to me with shit of confusion.

<u>Watchya man. I AM/WELL MY SON, YOUR NEPHEW IS A TESTAMENT THAT DNA IS A FRAUD.</u> I've proven this therefore, don't cross my spirit because; **from a EARTH PERSPECTIVE,** WE ALL SHARE THE SAME DNA. That's your life lesson for today.

EVERY HUMAN HERE ON EARTH SHARE THE SAME BC DNA. Listen, no, let me stap because mi spirit a get crass, and crasser. Iron, magnesium, potassium, fleshy, or earthly make up.

Wha wrong with unnu BC Black People? Stop seeking acceptance from other cultures.

A suh unnu fool, fool that another nation can tun unnu inna ediat. No, don't answer that. **MAN'S SO CALLED HOLY BIBLE IS A TESTAMENT TO THE SHIT UNNU ACCEPT TO BE THE TRUTH OF LIFE.**

Therefore, hundreds of million of you; your name is truly not in the God's Book of Good, and True Life.

Unnu done.

Bleeping ediat.

Mama forgive me, but are you sure my younger brother is from you?

MY WORLD OF DREAMS 2019 – BOOK THREE - TIRADE

Im drap from di sky?

Mama, im ha sight, so why isn't he using his sight in the right, and proper way?

Yes, I went off reckless and rude, but I had to vent mom. Had to show the world just how bitter I am when it comes to this man, and what he did to you, and my grandmother.

I acknowledge him not, so why is my brother so accepting of him? Di man fool up yu madda. Im not even tun im back pan yu. So why would I accept him, and his lineage? You never lost anything in life not knowing him. You lived good and true without him.

You never craved a father; him. At least you never said while you were alive.

I know him not. You mummy is all I know. You raised us right. We never inquired of him when we were younger, so why is my fool, fool brother keeping his name, and heritage alive?

Why want or need acceptance from people who know you not, or even care about you? Leave them the hell alone because; they are condemned, as well as condemned by me. I acknowledge his people not.

If I am wrong mom, please forgive me, but I need no acceptance from him, or his people, ancestors, or heritage.

MY WORLD OF DREAMS 2019 – BOOK THREE - TIRADE

I am truly happy the way I am. You were never short of true love in your life because; your batty neva touch grung. I truly love you, therefore; set my brother straight, and tell him not to provoke me with the Syrian bullshit, because I will never accept this lineage for you, and me. I know differently hence, I know Lovey. And you Lovey, need to set the lying White Race based on hue straight. Dem too bleeping lie, and deceiving.

Tell me Lovey; A wi di Black Race yu ha strength fa?

Si wi cum deceive wi stamp pan wi forehead?

A suh wi tun fool fi other race (s), and culture?

I am truly proud of my Jamaican roots and culture nuh matta how mi cuss di people dem. Dem too fool, fool.

ACCEPT YOU FOR WHO YOU ARE.

BE PROUD OF YOU.

DO NOT GIVE UP YOUR ROOTS AND CULTURE TO ACCEPT ANYONE'S ROOTS AND CULTURE AS YOUR OWN WHEN IT'S NOT. MEANING, IF THAT CULTURE IS TRULY NOT YOURS, DO NOT ACCEPT IT.

<u>*Lovey, what's wrong, and truly wrong with Black People globally?*</u>

You Lovey is too bleeping calm when it comes to them; White People based on hue, and based on hue and evil deeds as of 2019. Their lies, and deceit must stop because it does hurt. I am hurting, and you know this, but as of late you've been dormant, and I am simply tired of this.

How the hell can you be my good up, good up, and let me hurt by this shit of DNA?

Do you truly care about me?

You asked me to do something, and I am doing it, yet; you would rather see me hurt, and tormented in life.

Now tell me, where is your good, and true respect of me?

TRUTH; have you forgotten this Lovey?
Do you truly love the lies here on earth?

Do you like to see me in pain?

<u>**Or**</u>

ARE YOU JUST PISSED OFF THAT I AM HAPPILY DANCING TO A BEAUTIFUL SONG? **Good Cry** *by J. Boog and Chaka Demus.*

MY WORLD OF DREAMS 2019 – BOOK THREE - TIRADE

You can't stand to see me happy, and that's truly a shame on your part.

Know this Lovey, and to piss you off. ***I WANT THE GOOD CRY.*** Wait, you good, because I am just taking in the song when J. Boog said, "they can't get along." Plus when she wake up angry. Lovey, yu good, because my brother called, and mash up my good up good up vibe with his DNA bullshit.

I have to give you this Lovey. Yu noa fi push mi button, an a long time mi nuh go off reckless an rude pan yu.

Thank you, and have a wonderful day and night because; I am ending this book now.

Michelle

Before I close this book; it's February 13, 2019, and I dreamt these things.

Dreamt Vybz Kartel, and Ninja Man. Dreamt they were being transported in this open back truck/van/jeep. Vybz Kartel was sitting to the left of me, and Ninja Man was sitting on the right of me as I was facing West, and the direction they were going in was west.

Neither Vybz Kartel, or Ninja Man spoke to each other, and I said to them no fighting. I did not want them to start fighting/killing each other.

Oh man, I forgot; they were in handcuffs. I distinctly saw handcuffs on Vybz Kartel. So I do not know if these two will be collaborating musically.

No, I doubt that, but then you never know. Vybz Kartel is in prison, and he's still recording music. Hence bad man run the prison system of Jamaica. Prison is just a front for those who have money; well are in so-called jail, yet can record music while behind bars.

Only in Jamaica people because; **the WICKED, AND CORRUPT RUN TINGS.**

MONEY TALK, AND ALL OTHERS HAVE TO WALK. HEY, MONEY BUY YOU ANYTHING IN JAMAICA. Hence, Jamaica is also the pedophile capital of the world.

MY WORLD OF DREAMS 2019 – BOOK THREE - TIRADE

Politicians are so corrupt and evil dat; money can buy dem literally, stamp inna dem han, packet book, bank account, forehead, and peep, peep; penis because none have balls; are not men and woman that have good morals, and moral values.

Hey, if you have money, whatever you want………let me stop because mi chat tu much. But know, money run things in Jamaica. Hence, the land; no, the people are corrupt; hence many dirty cops, and politicians. Lord, I won't even touch on the clergy of the land.

Have mercy because I am dreaming about my teeth again. In the dream, I was looking at my teeth, and they were yellow, and I woke up out of my sleep.

Yes, death for me. Let's hope it's not me. My body is in too much pain people, and these muscle spasms that are painful, is getting to me, not to mention my back pain.

Need some Vitamin S.

No, not sex for you Jamaicans, but Sun. Need to replenish my Vitamin D therefore, I need to go someplace warm where I can lay in the sun, and get my Vitamin S.

Sun vitamin people, or Vitamin Sun. Yes, corny I know.

Did I dream me being on another planet?

Yes, and Data from Star Trek was in the dream. So, I truly do not know if there is going to be another Star Trek show, reboot, movie.

Yea me if there is another Star Trek movie coming out real soon.

In the dream, it was family; this one hideous guy that went after his family; brother to kill him.

So yes, more family members here on earth are going to feud. Let's hope this feud skips my family, but then I am not immune to conflict.

Well yes, I am. I will not fight with family for anything. I said my peace with my brother above in this book with his Syrian nonsense. I guess he doesn't know that some Italians are descendants of Arabs; that side of the Babylonian chain and or, mixture. Hence some are called "Sand Niggers," as told to me by an Italian.

Listen everyone, I have to respect my mother, and grandmother. Her father; my mother truly did not know. I never met this man. All there is is pure mystery. I truly do not think of him; my mother's father. If I was to give any thought to him, I would be disrespecting my mother, and grandmother, and condoning what he did to my mother, and grandmother, and I cannot do that; condone him and his wrongs; blatant hatred of my gorgeous and beautiful mother, and grandmother.

<u>*For me, and to me; from a father abandon his child, fool up im baby madda, im hate them; mother and child, more than unconditionally.*</u> The same goes for some mothers. If you do not want children, or can't afford to take care of a child; **DO NOT HAVE ANY.** It is a sin to have children you cannot take care of, and you are sinned. This sin also goes for women who have children for money, murderers, and so forth.

My brother is not me. **<u>I cannot be happy for a lineage I know nothing about. Nor can I accept this man.</u>** If I accepted this man, and his lineage; I would be condoning the evils he did to my mother, and grandmother. I cannot accept him therefore, I will never condone what he did to my gorgeous and beautiful mother, and grandmother.

<u>*He never knew her; therefore, I cannot know him, or want, or need anything of him including his blood, and lineage.*</u>

Therefore, let him keep his space, and place in hell because I am locking the door to his hell more than infinitely and indefinitely, and more than forever ever without end with him in it.

Kick rocks because MI CHUA MI SHOES AT YU, AN PAN YU. We are officially divorced forever ever without end. Your heritage and lineage can never ever be mine because; I did truthfully denounce, and divorce you in the wickedest of ways. I used *my dirty shoes therefore, disrespecting you, your heritage, lineage, and culture.*

If my siblings want to acknowledge you, it's up to them, but I refuse to.

My mother is my true star, and queen.

And yes, I know I will be hated globally, but hey, it's life. Many do not want to know the truth hence billions live in lies, as well as live for lies.

My life, god, truth, mother, family is truly important to me. I have to respect my mother, and no one is going to get me to disrespect her.

Respect is due to her, and I am respecting her to more than the max. Keep goodness and truth in your life all the time, and I am keeping my goodness; my Mother and Lovey fi real.

MICHELLE

It's Valentine's Day, and I am at my father's apartment. I slept so wonderfully. Beautiful sleep for me compared to my 2018 sleep state.

Happy Valentine's Day everyone.

As Black History Month continue – Happy Black History Month.

As for my dreams. Dreamt I was on an airplane, and the plane was dormant. Was not going anywhere. We were stuck in limbo. You could see this White Female Stewardess standing at the front of plane while passengers were sitting. **She said nothing.** This other female stewardess I was talking to then; she spoke to someone else about lunch. The dream is weird people because at one point of the dream, **we were flying but we weren't**; we were in limbo on the tar mac. Again commercial flying came into play for me.

So yes, flying is an issue for me due to safety.

Dreamt my teeth again.

Dreamt, I was in the hospital with another ailment. Before I was released my tooth on my upper left side of my mouth came into play. This White Female Nurse was upset/angry at me due to the state of my teeth. She fixed it with this pink thing. Trust me, she took good care of my tooth.

Yes my tooth is still crap despite my dentist prescribing me antibiotics, and pain killers. Have to get deep cleaning done, and I am not sure of this because my tooth is in a bad state. So the spiritual realm is truly not happy with what's happening with my teeth. I truly hope all goes well for me next month when I get my deep cleaning done. It also looks as if my tooth is cracked. Therefore, I truly have to wonder what this dentist did when he was drilling my teeth before he filled it.

I also hope all goes well with my father next week because he's getting a colonoscopy done.

I do not know why your body have to decay internally when you get older. This is for me people. I have to deal with so much pain, and if it's not one thing it's the other. **Pain sucks.** My pain limit me, and I truly do not like to be limited period. So truly take care of your health. Take nothing for granted when it comes to your health. Keep on top of it so that when you are older, you do not have aches, and pain like me.

Did I dream Shaquille O'Neal?

Yes

In the dream, he got a script for a movie. Meaning he was slated to do a movie because he signed the contract for the movie. This young boy; white boy was teasing Shaq about the movie he was going to do. In the dream, you could not see the white boy, but it was implied the child was white.

He; the white boy was also teasing Shaq about money. Saying he needed money that was why he was doing the movie. In the dream it seemed like Shaq was doing another movie similar to Shazam.

With the white boy telling Shaq about money I jumped in and say, he needed money and that is why he was doing the movie.

Shaq said; he did not need the money. In the dream; Shaq had real estate; multiple homes.

At any rate; with me teasing Shaq, he came after me, and I was spelling his name when his ex-wife showed up. Suffice it to say, I got mumbled up when spelling Shaq's name in the dream. **I could not spell his name properly.**

With Shaq's ex-wife showing up. She had this brown dog with her. Think small dog. Those new small breed pit bull's they have. But this dog was not fierce; though the belly looked hungry; as if it needed food. (Brown dog with a bit of yellow in it, if I remember correctly.)

I forgot what I said; but Shaq said they; him and his ex-wife are friends and or, have a close relationship. In the dream, they were not enemies people.

All this was happening outside Shaq's home.

Now we were inside the house, and Soldier Boy the rapper was now in the dream. There was some kind of discussion going on, and Shaq's ex-wife was getting intimate with Soldier Boy with Shaq, and me there. She was touching him on his breast. I so can't remember if Soldier Boy had a nipple ring. But she; Shaq's ex wife was all up on Soldier Boy.

Shaq was not fazed by this. He just said; I'm going to leave you two alone. Some thing to that affect because, I cannot remember word for word what Shaq said. All you see was Shaq leaving. I believe his ex-wife Shanice went into another direction; room as well. But with Soldier Boy being in the room, Shaq had an adjoining room that led back to the room Soldier Boy was in. So Shaq went through one door only to come back into the same room Soldier Boy was in.

When Shaq came back into the room, he beat the crap out of Soldier Boy. Man did he Shaq do some serious damage to him. To the way Shaq was beating up Soldier Boy; part's of Soldier Boy's body became mush. I say mush because the state of Soldier Boy was graphic; meaning, his body was coming apart to the way Shaq beat the crap out of him. When you say ass whooping; what Shaq did to Soldier Boy was beyond a ass whooping. It was sadistic; no, beyond sadistic. I cannot tell you what else Shaq did to this young man because, it's too sadistic. What I can tell you is, it had to do with an object; fire extinguisher and Soldier Boy's bum bum.

MY WORLD OF DREAMS 2019 – BOOK THREE - TIRADE

Then Shaq's ex-wife came into the room with two swords. Think Aladdin swords. She brought the swords in to give to Soldier Boy for him to use on Shaq.

Was one of the swords bigger than the other that Shanice brought in?

Yes.

I will not analyze this dream because I truly do not know what to make of it. But Shanice to ha man in front of Shaq anna kiss im tu. Gyal yu brave. An inna di man ouse tu.

Yu braver dan brave to regile.

Soldier Boy, I truly do not….let me leave it because this dream truly do not concern me.

Wow

And, to jump ahead of Book Four. I dreamt Shaq doing more than one (1) commercial. He had 2-3 going.

So Shaq truly look into your finances. Seriously look into it because something is not right with your money situation.

I know many rich people are going to lose their finances; money, so ensure yours is secure for what's to come. You have the heads up, so truly listen.

In another dream you were showing your ass. So, stop showing your ass because it's that fine. Hence, I did an ode to it; your ass. Your fine ass is mine. I claim it because it's truly beautiful in my world. Yes, I want to touch it.

Will you let me?

Damn boy that ass.

Yes!!!!!!!!!!!!!!!!!!!!

Also dreamt Floyd Mayweather.

Damn he's a showboat for real when it comes to money.

In the dream, he paid his female assistants extremely well. The females he had around him ensured he was secure in life, and had all he needed hence; they got paid very well. This is a know fact in real life.

Think payment in the millions for some of his female assistants. In the dream they had absolutely nothing to worry about. Basically, **<u>in the dream; Floyd used money to get what he wanted. In the dream; If he Floyd needed a woman, he would use his money to get her, and that's what he did in the dream.</u>**

All around him were secure financially.

In the dream, it was also implied that he Floyd wanted me; tried to use his money to get me, but I was not interested in him, or his money. But that was not the odd part of the dream. The odd part of the dream was; the crowd of people that was in the dream, and Floyd was throwing money into the crowd. Family and people; my true family, **the man threw away ONE HUNDRED AND FIFTY MILLION DOLLARS in the crowd.** Also, it was implied that one of his female assistant got paid fifteen million dollars.

I will not analyze this dream either. This man is a damned show boat; squanders money too much. Therefore, I do not know if he's going to lose over one hundred and fifty million dollars shortly to the way he was throwing away money. I know I said I was not going to analyze this dream.

Sorry everyone. But to the way some Black People have money to just throw it away on stupidity is beyond me.

Instead of buying females; their vagina, spend some of your money on Black People who need help. Buy some fixer uppers houses, and fix some up, and donate these fixer uppers to your own black brothers and sisters in the United States that need help; housing.

Yes, I know it's not my money, and it's his; Floyd's money, but it does piss me off to see the recklessness of some of our people when it comes to money. Therefore, I cannot, and will never ever *feel sorry for any that lose it all. When you have it, secure your future.*

Remember your old age, and sickness in old age. Some of us get sick, and what you saved, you have to spend on getting better. So think wise, and put away money for sickness, and old age. Yes, I want to say more, but I am going to leave things as is.

You know what; let me stay out of this, because it truly do not concern me. I truly love to give people. Let it go Michelle.

True love always people, and Happy Valentine's Day. May this day be great, happy, and filled with lots of flowers, chocolate, good food, good eating, good sex, good and true love for everyone that is good and true, as well as in a good, true, and clean relationship.

I forgot a dream.

You know what forget it.

Michelle

BOOKS WRITTEN BY MICHELLE JEAN 2019

My World of Dreams 2019 – Book One
My World of Dreams 2019 – Book Two